WHAT'S IN YOUR HAND?

By

Ayita Burks

HeartLife Publications
Hazel Crest, Illinois

WHATS IN YOUR HAND?

By Ayita Burks

Published by:
HeartLife Publications
Post Office Box 680
Hazel Crest, IL 60429
proverbs31cjw@yahoo.com

Library of Congress Control Number: 2023920759

ISBN-13: 978-0-9791120-4-1

Printed in the United States of America.

HeartLife Publications Mission Statement:

That I may publish with the voice of thanksgiving, and tell of all thy wondrous works.

Psalm 26:7, KJV

HeartLife Publications is established to challenge everyone to develop a genuine relationship with God that is built on a true confession of faith in Christ Jesus and supported by a godly lifestyle.

CONTENTS

Introduction

I have spent years in a financial struggle that has kept me stunted in my natural and spiritual growth. There, I said it! It feels good to get it off my chest verbally. However, this confession does not erase the constant reminder that I can't seem to move forward from a lifetime of bad decisions and habits. I want to change, and I know that the Bible has instructions. Even further, it says that God wants us to have an abundant life (John 10:10), but I realize that my current circumstances are not plentiful. What can I do? I usually start with prayer and the Word of God, but what am I missing?

I—like you—have to ask myself: What am I *not* doing? God gives us many answers that require faith and direct obedience. For each of us to receive the response we seek, the healing we need, and the next step in the story, we need to act. This action is not to be taken without the direction of God, but I firmly believe that God doesn't give us every single step of the plan.

I find many lessons from the stories of the people that followed God in the Bible. For the solution in this book, God reminded me of a story in the Bible where a woman had a significant financial problem. The problem was so big that her creditors wanted to imprison her children due to her husband's debt. The most crucial step that the widow took was to seek out God's wisdom. Let me point out that there were many steps she could have taken to solve her problem. There are dishonorable ways to create money and criminal methods to get money, but many new problems arise with these choices. Even more complicated methods take lots of time and utilize much-needed resources. However, only God's solution has the guarantee of His resources and power. Yes, seeking and obeying God may take work on your part; but your betterment and peace are never at stake.

In *What's in Your Hand?* I take an in-depth look at this biblical woman and her family. I also look at the widow's process in order to provide a template for financial freedom. As I do this, I hope that every reader that needs a swift kick in the action "tutti" will be able to have a plan for changing their life. I write this book as a case study from the Word of God. I believe strongly that it will be an asset in your journey to become free from bondage and overcome anything that is stopping you from getting to the promises of God.

As you read these pages, make sure you take time to review the scripture references. As you read these chapters, make sure you try to apply the lessons from this story to your life. As you read this book, allow God to use one person's experience to change your life. Then, when you establish victory over your situation, please share your story with others to enable them to be free. Finally, I pray that reading this book will encourage you to take time to strengthen your relationship with Christ and to exercise the measure of faith that God has given you.

As we begin this journey together, I want to whisper this revelation or reminder into your spirit as you read these words:

God wants you to be free, so you can set others free!

Suit up, soldier!

There's a Situation

Debt, slavery, and death are toxic combinations. In 2 Kings 4:1-38, we find the story of a woman facing a bit of each one. Let's take a minute to break down the facts! We know that her spouse has died, and she is a mother who has unpaid debt and no income. She is living in a time when the reign of the great King David and King Solomon is over, and Israel and Judah are separate. She is living in a time of fighting among kings and nations. She is living in a time when a woman's status is calculated by who her husband is. This widow's story starts with a situation that unbalanced her comfort and shook her stability. It sounds like the opening scene for the next Lifetime movie.

Her debt has left the widow in need of assistance from an outside source, like a relative or friend. We wonder why she cannot go to her family. All we know is that she does not. Maybe they have judged her, supposing that she or her husband had done something wrong to bring about God's wrath—like Job's friends thought that his calamity must have been the result of wrongdoing on his part (Job 4:23). What we do know is that the nature of this debt was overwhelming. We also know that the woman had friends or family around because later we see that her sons had to borrow vessels from them. So we know that, initially, to seek family support is not where the woman goes.

Although I am not a mother, I am an "auntie!" I would cross hell and high water for my niece and nephews. I'm not even the best auntie! Technically that would be either my sister Keshia or Claudia, my sister-in-love's sister. This widow was a mother. The devastation she must have felt to see her children put into a destitute position is heartbreaking. And think of the heartless creditor relentlessly out to make money at the expense of this poor family.

Even more, her husband had been a student of the prophet Elisha and was a man who feared God. This is the straw that breaks the camel's back! Have you ever found yourself saying, "Why God? I follow you. Why isn't this working to my advantage? Why do the heathens prosper, but my family lacks what it needs? Heaven help me!" As I type, I feel the widow's mind trying to make sense of everything. Death, debt, and destruction reared their ugly faces to the widow. They robbed her of solutions, probably even prevented her from asking for outside help, and deprived her of the hope that could have been found in her son's future provision for the family.

Finally, I see the challenge to her belief. Everyone in their community could see that the family was in debt. They may have wondered, "How could the God that the widow's family served not take care of the situation? Why had He not allowed them to foresee this? I mean, didn't her husband follow the prophet? Wasn't he devoted?" It was not that different from how people would react today. I can see elements of my situation in their tragedy. How about you? Thankfully, this is not where the widow's story ended, and it's not where yours will end.

Take a moment to Reflect

Write your thoughts, questions, or what you have learned in this chapter:

Seek the Kingdom of God

Matthew 6:33 says, "But seek first the kingdom of God and His righteousness, and all these things will be added to you" (NKJV). This story could have been entirely different if the widow had decided not to seek God first. Alternate solutions and conclusions are endless. But would those options have put her in direct contact with the living God? In this section, we will look at the believers' road to seeking the kingdom of God; it starts with choice, continues with understanding the process, and ends in faith and action.

In this instance, the widow had to choose where to seek her information. The widow sought the God of Abraham. She decided to go to the proven prophet of God. She accepted all that the prophet said, trusting that it was from God.

The first chapter of the book of Proverbs states, "The fear of the Lord is the beginning of knowledge" (v. 7). I have dwelled on this scripture and thought about how important it is for the believer to begin all decisions here. For the believer, fearing God is not scary; it is powerful because you recognize who God is first. You recognize His power, authority, truth, and His way. You realize what He has already done first. This realization should be the starting point of every significant choice that the believer makes because the believer is conscious of what it means to make a decision apart from God.

The Bible doesn't explain how broad the widow's understanding of God was, but we do know that she knew who her husband followed. She probably had heard stories about Elijah and what God had done through him, and she knew that Elisha was a direct student of that mighty man of God. The stories about Elijah and Elisha still baffle the minds of Christians today. So one can imagine how awe-inspiring this must have been during the widow's lifetime.

Now that we have the foundation, let's look at the simple building blocks of where, who, and what. I had to ask myself, "Where am I seeking to find the answer to my situation or problem? Am I starting with God?" Pause here for a second. Here's a more challenging question: Do you really want God's answer? As I thought about this question, chills went up my spine.

There is a potency in God's solution to your situation that is beyond any self-development or guru's answer. It doesn't have to take a long time to come either; but I firmly believe that your willingness to receive His answer changes the timing. Just think, the children of Israel could have gone into the promised land but instead wandered for 40 years in a desert due to their disobedience. Many died before they could make it to what was promised. Some made it to the promise but were deceived through fear (see Numbers 13). Instead, they didn't understand the powerful God that walked them through the Red Sea. Even as I type these words, I feel the weight of this because I have reached my 43rd year and I am finally starting to write words to publish. So I ask you, "Do you really want God's answer?"

Because she wanted God's answer, the widow went to the scary prophet who called out judgment on the kids that mocked him (see 2 Kings 2:23-24). In those days, you hoped to be on the good side of what real prophets had to say when they spoke. What Elisha said came to pass. I love the fact that fear did not stop the widow. As a result, she became assured by God and by the servant that God sent His message through.

Today, believers have the benefit of the Bible which the widow did not have. She had to rely on her husband's training and the circulating stories. Today's believers can reside in the Word of God, patiently learning who God is and understanding what He would say and not say. Believers today don't have to wait for a word of God to come from a prophet, but they can be blessed if the prophet confirms what God says He is going to do. Today's believer has the benefit of a personal relationship with God. In this daily walk, the believer learns the ebb and flow of

God's character and actions. Therefore, believers can understand God's voice and "a stranger they will not follow" (John 10:5, KJV).

The stage is set to move into actively seeking God. When actively seeking God, you have received the directive, and now it is time to apply faith to what you have heard from God. Starting with your belief in God's truth, you are at war with every part of your inward feelings and outward flesh. Your inconsistencies, bad habits, and fears will rise to the occasion to make you doubt what God has to say. You will fight against the devil's suggestions to abort your decision to trust God's promise. (We will talk later about this in chapter 4 when we look at the plan God gave to the widow.) As you actively seek the kingdom of God, you will find that you are positioning yourself to obey what God is asking you to do.

In my experience, I have often found myself waiting for God to do something without readying myself for God's directive. There have been times that I missed out on the blessing because of my disobedience. I had to hope for the next chance. But at the end of the day, here is my favorite encouragement: As long as you are breathing and looking to God, it ain't over! God still has a purpose and a plan for you (Jeremiah 29:11).

Before I conclude this chapter, I want to stress the importance of the action of fervently seeking God and doing what He says by looking at examples from two parables from the Bible. In Luke 15:8-10, Jesus talked about a woman that lost 1 of the 99 coins she possessed. She searched her whole house looking for the one coin that she had lost. She overturned couches and tables to find this lost possession in her search. She did this with determination, without inhibition, and with an "I will find it!" attitude.

The second parable in Matthew 25:1-13 is a story of ten virgin bridesmaids who were waiting for their groom. Five of these ten young women readied themselves and their resources in preparation for the bridegroom and their wedding ceremony even though they didn't know when he would arrive. The other five maidens did not prepare themselves; and when it was time for them to meet their bridegroom, they were not married and missed out. The girls who fervently prepared for the groom displayed the important lesson of preparing for the eventuality. With both parables in mind, consider what lessons you can learn from the actions of these women as you consistently seek God for every answer, decision, vision, and plan you have to make.

Take a moment to Reflect

Write your thoughts, questions, or what you have learned in this chapter:

What's in Your Hand?

The widow's situation robbed her of the truth of what was in her hand. In response to Elisha's question, "What's in your house?" the widow said, "Nothing . . . but a jar of oil" (2 Kings 4:2). The widow didn't realize the strength of her relationships, the reality of her resources, and the power in her resolve. After looking at what was in the widow's hand, it will be your turn to look at what you have in your hand.

In my initial reading of 2 Kings 4:1-7, I completely missed the deeper connection that the widow had to Elisha. In the first verse, the widow states, "*Your servant,* my husband is dead." Her husband had directly served Elisha. The widow also says, ". . . *you know* that *your servant* feared the Lord" (v. 1). So how did I miss this crucial part of the relationship? The widow wasn't a random person to Elisha. She knew him, and he knew her through her husband. So she had direct communication with the direct representative of God. Even though she thought she had nothing in her house, this widow had two things: knowledge of God and connection to God's true representative.

I have read stories about Elisha and how the power of God flowed through his ministry. I read what happened when people came against him. To sum it up, it did not go well. The widow could come to Elisha with her concerns and problems and have his complete attention. This observance brings me to a second revelation: The widow's husband was in good standing with Elisha. This standing is one more thing that she had in her house.

God forgives and may even forget. Many times, people try to forgive but they seldom forget. They remember the character that you portrayed the first time, and this portrayal is what sticks. For many years, I have tried to be the most honest and trustworthy person to my dad; yet whenever I fail, he goes back to believing that he can't trust anything I have to say. His lack of confidence in my character hurts me deeply every time it comes up. I can have years of triumph right before his eyes, and he will always lean toward my failings. It might be something as simple as missing the time I am supposed to bring back the car and not fully communicating it to him. Then I am back at square one. My respectability comes into question. Thankfully, now we talk a little more about this. I even mention my shortcomings.

When the widow comes to the prophet, she could confidently say about his student, "he served you." Elijah didn't refute it. He replied, "What can I do for you?" There is power in the ability to come before God's representative boldly.

Fast forward to today, the Bible states that we can "come boldly unto the throne of grace, that we may obtain mercy, and find grace to help in time of need" (Hebrews 4:16, KJV). For the believer, this is immediate access. There is no call waiting, and God is always listening. Yes, we may have to be patient because God's timing is perfect, but this is part of the process as God resolves the issues of our lives. There is so much power in this part of the believer's relationship with the Creator.

Now, let's add the power of resolve. This widow was determined to find the answer and set on doing whatever it took. She was determined to obey God no matter what He wanted her to do. Like others who have exerted extraordinary faith that changed the course of human history, this widow utilized the same. The widow was determined to stand on the word that proceeded out of the prophet's mouth to save her whole family. Her resolve was to exercise complete obedience. This resolve is what this woman was working with. This resolve is what was in her hand. There is nothing little in that.

Now I ask you, "What's in *your* hand?" There is a reality that you see. You feel that you have nothing. An adversary is trying to take everything that you own. Your energy is not high. You may not have food or shelter. You may be sick. You may have lost your loved ones. You may be losing your life. Like the widow, embrace this reality of the little that you have.

This circumstance is the starting point of your story. This point is the mile marker of your journey. You don't have to think yourself out of it by thinking positively. You don't have to use realizations and vision boards. As some will say, you do not have to "fake it until you make it." What I am encouraging you to do today is to open your hand to God. Be honest with Him. Be willing to accept His help. Recognize His infinite power. Feed on His wisdom. Take Him at His word and stand on it. This relationship is what's in the believer's hand—access to God. What's in the believer's hand is an audience with the Creator of the entire universe. For the believer, there is the atonement (your sin covered by Jesus' blood) to reconnect you to God.

I write to those who are experiencing the death and destruction of their faith. I write to whomever is experiencing a battle for the visions and promises that God has given. I write to the one who has tried all they can do and is still finding that the walls of their world are crumbling. No matter where you are, remember that you are working with more than you see currently. You may feel that there is nothing in your storehouse but a little faith, a little oil, a little money, a little creativity, a little hope, a little love, a little . . ., etc. That's okay. Bring your little to the Lord and be willing and obedient to the plan He is about to lay out for you.

Now, with every encouragement towards God I also want to share a caution: Be careful that you do not become distracted. Stay focused on God's will and way. You see, it's easy to see the everyday, natural, worldly solutions that seem quick and satisfying. I'm not talking about the natural things that need to be done—like keeping your home clean or eating daily. I am talking about parasitic, worldly solutions that feed off your hopes, needs, resources, and fears. You have seen them:

> You got debt? Get this loan.
>
> Need comfort? Eat this.
>
> Need hope? Come to this seminar and pay for this 50-day course.

Understand that sometimes these things have their place, but God's way trumps all. Outside of God's will and way, you pay more, waste more time, and won't achieve the relationship and fellowship with God that you desperately need.

So, what's in your hand? God wants it. Open your hand to God and watch Him unroll a master plan that will change your life.

Take a moment to Reflect

Write your thoughts, questions, or what you have learned in this chapter:

The Plan

The plan seemed simple enough: Borrow vessels, go into your house, close the door, and pour the oil. Why wouldn't anyone try this process? Precisely, right? Easy, right? But the widow had no idea about what was going to happen.

Let's look at what God spoke to her through Elisha. In 2 Kings 4:3, Elisha tells the widow to borrow vessels. The direct instructions were to borrow vessels from everywhere—from all your neighbors. Elisha states that they must be empty vessels. They had to be ready. This instruction is smart! We do not know if the vessels were small, medium, or large; but they had to be empty. The wiggle room about shape, size, and type presents one of those gray areas that could get some of us stuck. We strive for perfection in the minor details when God wants us to focus on the function of what He asks. Selah: pause and think about it.

Let's also think about how this instruction would apply to us today. Vessels are readily accessible in America at our local Walmart or even in the nearest thrift store. But before you reach for the next quick solution, think more about what is already in your possession. Today's vessels may look like the blank pieces of paper in front of you. The vessel can be the computer's word processing program that you type your thoughts into. A vessel today may be equipment that enhances your creativity—the recorder you speak into, the empty canvas to paint on, or maybe even the beginning materials for a new creation. The vessel can be as simple as wherever the thought will be contained and well-protected within its container.

Let's go even further to say that the containers of today look more like: a budget (how much money you have and what to use it on), funding (how much money you raise), planning (what's done, who does it, and when it is done), a vision (what the end product looks like), human resources (obtaining and maintaining the people who make it possible), a marketing strategy (where it's sold, who it's sold to, when it's sold, how it's sold, and how it's communicated), service (maintaining how people interact with the oil), etc.

The vessel gives the oil protection, shape, order, size, and reality. The vessel becomes the conduit for bringing about the miracle. Just think, the vessel was essential and specific to what God would do. The vessels needed to be empty and ready. These vessels couldn't have cracks or holes because of what they would be holding. The vessels could not be weak because they needed to contain something of value. There had to be many vessels because God is infinite. But you and I are limited; so we need the vessels.

"Do not borrow a few" was the next directive from Elisha. What a task for the widow: Go borrow *many* vessels from your neighbors and friends. So now she had to get a lot. Within this task, we find another gray area that could have stopped the widow. There was no timeframe on how long she would need these vessels. Usually, when you are borrowing something from a friend or neighbor, they want to know the how long you will need it and why. I can almost hear the conversation, "So, what are you using my jars for? A miracle? How long will that take?" The disapproving stares would have halted me in my tracks.

Based on this story, many neighbors might have leased out their vessels because Elisha didn't give a timeframe. This is another gray area! How was the widow to know how long God would take? Okay, Elisha, now you're asking this poor widow to lower herself before her neighbors and friends to borrow their stuff—specifically, items they will probably need—and ask to keep it for an indefinite amount of time without them knowing the purpose? No wonder the widow delegated this task to her sons.

You have to give her points for delegating the work. When God provides us with a job, mission, goal, or dream, it is usually too big to conquer on our own. Knowing the importance of teamwork, networking, and community movement is essential to the mission. Indeed, this widow had much in her hand and within her abilities.

After gathering the resources needed, the widow had to bring the borrowed vessels into her house (2 Kings 4:4). Let's now talk about centralizing the effort. Have you ever tried to find the thought you wrote in one of your thousands of notebooks? Have you had that moment when you looked everywhere and still couldn't find the one thing you needed? You know that ingredient that is somewhere in the kitchen, but you are unsure if it is in a cabinet or refrigerator? God is the master of the centralized effort on our behalf. The instruction was not to be everywhere; it was to go home! Her home was the base for the effort and the place where the miracle would occur. At home is where the resources would be. The family would do the work at home. The important people were to gather there.

The oil, the widow, her sons, and the vessels are now in one place. The stage is set for God to do His amazing work. As you centralize your efforts for God's work, watch for things hindering its effectiveness. Some halters of your effort can be indecision, disobedience, confusion, and more. These distractions may cause you to miss God's specific instructions. (We will discuss this in the following chapters.) One tip you can use is to pay attention to where God wants you to centralize.

For the widow, it was right at home. Home—this location was readily available, at the lowest cost, and familiar to the widow. The people involved understood the possibilities and limitations of the location. Each person involved understood how to prepare the home for function. Because the directive from God was to collect many vessels, the widow had to prepare a place in her home to store these vessels. There also needed to be room to do their household and work activities. I'm sure pathways were cleared in the house for the widow to obey the orders from God.

Now, let's talk about the inner work of centralizing your heart and mind. The widow was determined to follow the instructions of God. If this were not her position, the miracle would not have happened, she would not have prepared her home, nor would she have followed every instruction. The widow's determination to obey God was the birthing ground for doing the work to centralize the family's efforts. The widow and her family trusted God as the authority, which was another way the widow prepared her heart and mind to do what was required.

I have thought about what trusting God means. Trusting is so hard to do at times. It begins in the decision area of our hearts and minds. God made us intelligent, and we have power and ability from the living God inside of us. We can do what we put our minds and hands to do. But trusting God isn't assuming that we can do anything. Trusting requires relinquishing confidence in our ability in order to focus on the desires and actions of the one we trust. If God wants it, we go for it. If He doesn't, we stop. Trusting God is an issue of the heart because it involves battling with your will in response to God's. Sometimes science or circumstances may back up our will, but God understands all things. The human authority at hand may approve what we want as if it's okay; but if God doesn't want it, then we cease to want it. Trusting is hard but necessary for the believer to be ready for answers and miracles from God.

Finally, the widow prepared her heart to finish. She was going to endure to the end. Nothing was going to stop her from saving her family. She had come to the right source for the right plan, and now executing this plan was in her sight. Her effort became militarized. The stage was set spiritually, mentally, and physically for the miracle to begin.

Paying attention to this next part of the instruction is crucial to implementing what God wants to do. Once the resources and tools were in the house, the next instruction was to shut the door. In other words, nothing could come in or out. Stop for a moment and think about this. Why was this part so important? Why couldn't they keep the doors open for others to see God working this miracle? Why couldn't everyone know the process that was in motion?

First, let's point out that this miracle was only for the widow and her family. Second, God wants your attention on Him and nothing else. Shutting the door keeps all distractions away and the influences of any other god out. Another revelation is that everyone wants proof of God, but not everyone wants to come to God as He asks them to. Everyone wants the miracle without the process and authentic relationship with God.

The truth is we want our outcome as we see fit. The expected outcome becomes a god. We hear countless stories today where people are asking, "Why didn't God do this, stop this, or see this? Why doesn't He show up when you or I want Him?" In these cases, how many people truly live according to the God-breathed words that are in the Bible? Which ones have developed their personal relationship with God and accepted the gift of salvation? As a believer, is God's will more important than your will? How many that are on the outside looking in are champions of misinformation regarding God? Some may not agree with the thought process of God's will above all. However, God's way is the best way. Going another way will produce a result. Although it may seem favorable, it won't end in a relationship with the God of Abraham, Isaac, Jacob, David, and Jesus. He that has ears, let him hear!

The next part of the plan was for the widow to pour the oil. Elisha gives her the last instruction: ". . . then pour it into all those vessels, and set aside the full ones" (2 Kings 4:4). To act on blind belief is the scary part of crazy that non-believers fault Christians for and yet praise non-believers when they do. Hearing these words from the prophet could not have been easy. Scientifically, there was no sense in what Elisha was asking her to do. She could have stopped here because this instruction was impossible. It was scientifically unexplainable and, as outsiders would say, "outright stupidity." To anyone listening, the outsiders could have been right because it seemed that Elisha had lost his natural mind. Of course, no one would have said it out loud because this was Elisha! If he wanted you gone, you were out of the game. Selah!

What was undeniable was that she knew the prophet. She knew who he represented. And she knew that with God, impossibility is possible. Therefore, the widow could have complete trust that overrides all sense. (You know, you can too!) Her direct action would lead to the miracle that only she and her sons would witness.

I'm so thankful that the widow heard the plan and obeyed. And now the battle begins.

Take a moment to Reflect

Write your thoughts, questions, or what you have learned in this chapter:

Obedience: A Weapon of Faith

From the outside looking in, God's plan for the widow seemed easy. The steps weren't too crazy. The tasks seemed to be within the scope of what the widow and her family could do. The rest of the story is about the widow's obedience. Second Kings 4:5 states, "So she went from him, and shut the door upon her and upon her sons, who brought the vessels to her; and she poured out" (KJV). The widow did the most powerful thing a believer in the living God can do: She took God at His word and obeyed.

Obeying God is not for the faint of heart. It is war. It is a war against self. It's a war against circumstances and surroundings. Sometimes, it's a war between you and the people in your life—whether it be colleagues, friends, or even family. It's a war against comfort and fleshly desires. And if that wasn't enough, there is an ever-present enemy who continually seeks to halt the miracle of God in your life. Thankfully, there is much power in obeying God. This obedience is the same power that the forefathers and foremothers of faith used.

The power of obedience to God is instrumental in the war against self. As humans, we have a constant battle between spirit and flesh. Galatians 5:17 says, "For the flesh desires what is contrary to the Spirit, and the Spirit what is contrary to the flesh. They are in conflict with each other . . ." (NIV). God's Word also says that "the weapons of our warfare are not carnal, but mighty through God . . ." (2 Corinthians 10:4, KJV). Obeying God's Word becomes a mighty weapon in the believer's arsenal for use in everyday life. Let's look a little deeper at the part that obedience plays in the widow's story, and hopefully you will be able to see how to exercise this valuable weapon of your warfare.

The widow displayed obedience over timing. We see nothing in this story that alludes to the widow's hesitation. When Elisha gave the plan to the widow, she carried out each task strategically. There was no indication that the widow or her family were lazy or falling asleep regarding the tasks that needed completion. Diligence was part of the entire family's timely actions. You can tell that there was a sense of urgency due to the creditor's deadline; yet the widow and her family persevered within the time constraints that were at hand, not knowing if a miracle would happen. Here is where the teachable moment for every believer comes in: God producing a miracle does not negate the timeliness of the work on our part.

The widow exercised obedience over her surroundings and circumstance. Her circumstance was that she was a woman in a male-dominated society and her widowhood had shifted her income bracket. I'm sure people had heard that the debt collector was coming to take away her sons and make them slaves to pay her husband's debt (2 Kings 4:1). As soon as friends and family found out, they may have had something to say about what she needed to do. It can be quite an experience to be in front of multiple "know-it-alls!" But the widow continued with the plan in obedience to God. She did not add information or the advice and opinions of others to the task that God had directed. The widow didn't let the conversations of her family and friends get inside her head. She stayed obedient to God. She may have missed her husband tremendously, but she didn't allow the woe of the moment to dictate how obedient she would be. Although the circumstances had become dangerous to her family, she pushed her family to be obedient to God's plan.

Here is the part of obedience that the woman displayed that continues to blow my mind. She was obedient to God while the reality of her situation was impossible. There was only a little oil. There was no getting around this reality. She and her family saw this with their eyes. Therefore, they could have voided this plan before it started because logic dictates the parameters of any plan. The fact is: If you only have a little oil, there is no way to change the science of the outcome. It's basic mathematics. But God! She knew what God did through Elisha, and her family knew this because of the father's service. So, with faith she obeyed even though it was impossible.

Let's take a moment here to stop and consider this. Could you honestly say that you would be as quick and concise to implement the task of this plan? Knowing that it was impossible, would you be able to stop yourself from trying alternatives? Would you have the courage to obey, knowing it may not work? Or even more, what if the outcome was not the one that you would want? Would you be able to exert the same obedience? Just take a moment to think and pray about it because the wonderful thing is that you, believer, have a big God!

Next, I want to talk about the widow's obedience beyond that which was unseen. Ephesians 6:12 states, "For we wrestle not against flesh and blood, but against principalities, against powers, against the rulers of the darkness of this world, against spiritual wickedness in high places" (KJV). Being connected to Elisha, who truthfully followed God, gave much credibility to the widow's efforts. But it was not all a bed of roses; some rulers were against God's way. What about the leaders of the community where the widow lived? Could they have tried to halt the widow's efforts? Was the society of the time full of belief in God or did the people follow other gods?

There were a lot of changes to leadership in this time and there was persecution and the scattering of the people of God. The impact of politics and culture may have added to the story and thickened that plot, but the widow exercised obedience despite these obstacles—and the miracle happened.

Finally, let's talk about the devil's reign in this world and his suggestive power in our lives. The devil knows that the promises of God are true and wants to rob every believer of this truth continually. Knowing that a believer's relationship with God is the most important thing., the devil will work hard to suggest that you follow every other direction or relationship but this one. The devil's tactics are persuasive and addictive, and he will use every device and weapon to stop you from actively seeking God's will for your life. The devil works hard to bend the truth with suggestion and persuasion to help the believer doubt God. He starts with the specifics of what God said and manipulates your understanding and desire. We see many occurrences in the Bible where the devil uses half-truths and our misunderstandings to rob the believer of victory.

The widow was already ahead of most of the devil's deception by going to God first. She put a nail in the devil's coffin by following each step of the plan, down to each specific detail. The last and most important part was the widow's obedience to lead her and her family's efforts. The widow and her family poured the oil until the vessels were completely filled. I'm sure the devil fought until logic could no longer outweigh what was happening and the widow began to see the miracle. Maybe he continued to fight her and her family even as they continued pouring and were witnessing the miracle unfold before their eyes. His last-ditch effort may have been to try to stop them from filling the very last jar. But once there were no more jars to fill or oil to pour, there was nothing that he could do. Take that, devil!

Exerting action with faith is the hardest and scariest point of this process, but the widow conquered it with obedience to God. The widow won through obedience to God, and no one could take this from her and her family. Just think of the salvation of her family. Obedience is a battlefield, but God has already won the war!

God's work was done. Now, the real work began!

Take a moment to Reflect

Write your thoughts, questions, or what you have learned in this chapter:

God's Work Is Done; Now Yours Begins

The plan that God gave paid off. The miracle had tangible evidence. No one would have blamed the widow or her family if they had stopped there. The excitement would have made me blab to the whole world, "Look what God did, haters!!!" (This was not the action that the widow took, but "I'm just saying . . .!" Personally, I would not have been mad at her.) Instead, the widow returned to the man of God to let him know that the impossible became possible. Then the prophet told the woman what was next. From there, she was to go and sell the oil, pay the debt, and live off the rest (2 Kings 4:7b). The practical application of the miracle saved the woman's children and provided a life where they could thrive.

Christians today love the spiritual side of heaven. Once God does something, why do we think that a miracle always has to happen? We keep seeking the signs and wonders when God has passed the ball to us so that we can continue the work. It even says in the Word, "A wicked and adulterous generation seeketh after a sign; and there shall no sign be given unto it, but the sign of the prophet Jonas" (Matthew 16.4, KJV).

This widow didn't stay in the moment. She returned to life and sought direction from God's representative once again. She repeated the process with the same heart to work until she had what was needed. The lesson from the widow's actions is: Although God will do the miraculous, our lives should revolve more around our relationship with God and the work of His will. The widow returned to the practical application of God's will and would continue to work to gain the resources needed to change the outcome for her and her family. This work was fueled by the fact that the widow and her family knew that the miraculous had happened; and it was a story they would never forget.

The work of selling the oil was left to the practical application of business. There had to be a promotion (telling others that you have oil to sell), a sales process (where the consumer and seller meet), a transaction (exchange of monies, goods, or services), and budgeting (allotting money to the proper areas, such as paying the debt, establishing a new budget, and setting up a plan to thrive). These efforts must be done consistently, harmoniously, and with integrity. Paraphrasing Pastor Thaddeus Searcy from Freedom Church in Lansing, Illinois, "At this point, you are living in Proverbs!" In other words, you are applying practical knowledge and wisdom to all areas of your life. The real work had begun for the widow and her family; and they, hopefully, worked diligently.

I read an article by Tonja Murphy, faith columnist for the *Clarion Ledger,* who wrote, "The widow could have easily said, 'Forget the creditors,' and just lived. But instead, she again followed the instruction of the prophet to sell the oil, pay her debts, and then live. I've seen people receive financial blessings and forget their debts. The latest clothes, car, or gadgets top their lists. As a result, they deplete their blessings and circle back to God, receive correction in love, and change their behaviors when He blesses the next time."[1] I, Ayita Burks, have done this multiple times—heartbreaking times, devastating times! Thankfully, God is a redeeming God, and He is always faithful. So, I say to encourage you, the reader, "Believer, you are not alone. God can redeem you, too!"

The widow's story ends here without us knowing the rest. From her prior actions, one can sum up that she and her family did what was needed to bring about the wealth they needed, and they never repeated what brought them to such a dire state. The work was now in their hand.

Take a moment to Reflect

Write your thoughts, questions, or what you have learned in this chapter:

Next Level: Thrive

The debt was paid, wealth was at hand, and the worries were gone. Now what? It was time to live off the rest. Can you feel it? The weight was lifted, the air was clearer, and the possibilities had become almost endless. Now that the situation was over, the widow's subsequent decisions, habits, and actions could enhance or destroy the next part of her story.

As a blueprint for thriving, I encourage you to read Proverbs 3. Proverbs was primarily written by King Solomon, son of David. He was a king who had great wisdom, and peace was within his reign. When he wrote the book of Proverbs, it was from the perspective of talking to his children. It was likely a letter to instruct people in wisdom and righteousness. When reading Proverbs, you will find that when there is an instruction to do something, and there is also a statement about what will happen because of your obedience and disobedience. Although I encourage you to read about all of the effects of obedience, there are some points I will emphasize about living your life under the Proverbs 3 principles.

Proverbs 3:1 starts with, "My son, forget not my law; but let thine heart keep my commandments" (KJV). In other words, this statement says, "Remember what I have instructed you in son/daughter and put continual action to the rules I've given you for living." As you learn to thrive, there are godly rules, there are good rules, and there is what is just plain wrong. You will learn to discern between the good and the godly and stay away from the evil. Thankfully, the Bible has guidelines that are proven and undeniable. It shows how God does things; and even in good things it shows you the evil. It is your job, as you thrive, to keep insight and instruction from the Bible and what God has shown you in life as a compass for your actions and decisions. This is the foundation of thriving for you and your legacy.

Like the widow, you must start with coming to God first! Proverbs 3:3 states, "Let not mercy and truth forsake thee: bind them about thy neck; write them upon the table of thine heart" (KJV). One of the notes in the King James Version of the *Life Application Study Bible* states: "Two important character qualities are mercy and truthfulness. Both involve actions as well as attitudes. A merciful person not only feels love, but he also acts responsibly and faithfully. A truthful person not only believes in the truth; he also works for justice for others. Thoughts and words are not enough."[2] This note helped me understand how these attributes must become a part of my life. And as you and I take this to heart, we must then turn it into action.

The phrase "bind them about thy [your] neck" has always impacted me when I read this scripture. When I think of binding mercy and truth about one's neck, I think of the yoke on a horse or an ox. It is the mechanism that guides the direction of the animal. This direction is dependent on the driver. With God as the driver, truth and mercy come directly from the source. A thriving person will not let mercy and truth forsake him or her; instead, these qualities will be in full view.

Proverbs 3:5-6 states, "Trust in the Lord with all thine heart; and lean not unto thine own understanding. In all thy ways acknowledge him . . ." (KJV). Have you ever seen the rodeo where the bull is bucking, kicking, and even throwing the rider off? It is a sight to see! But you also see the fantastic things that happen when an animal trusts the rider's direction. Work gets done in fields, the rider can cover miles faster, and you even see where amazing jumps and leaps happen—all because the animal trusts its rider. It is so important to put your trust in God. You may know He is the ultimate authority, but you must trust Him—not another direction, not your way, only His! Refer to it, rely on it, obey it, and live or die by it. This is acknowledging God. It's another foundation of the thrive.

Proverbs 3:7 states, "Be not wise in thine own eyes: fear the Lord, and depart from evil" (KJV). I have to stay here for a little bit longer. This is where the shift comes: When you have the knowledge, resources, experience, and even power, you can envision where you want to go and what you want to do; and you can make it happen. Your opportunities are different at this point, and making decisions becomes more accessible. Options that are godly, good, or evil present themselves continually; and although good should win over evil, sometimes the godly choice takes a back seat. The wisdom you have achieved takes on its own life—if you let it—and it becomes the thing you rely on and base your actions and decisions upon.

At this point, you should always come back to the checkpoint of prayer, fasting, meditating on the Word of God, and keeping your eyes on Christ. Refrain from falling into the deceptions of past successes. Fear the Lord! He was there and built the very foundations of life. Respect the Lord, your God! His knowledge and way should be given priority. Reverence the Lord Jesus Christ; He is the Son of God! Depart from the tree of the knowledge of good and evil. Don't eat the apple, believer! Put yourself into the process of continually coming to the well of life and drink deeply from it. Life flows from this well. Our eyes can deceive us easily, but Jesus is the way, the truth, and the life (John 14:6). He came to give life and that life more abundantly (John 10:10). This doesn't mean that you cannot utilize your knowledge; but it does mean that the base of your belief is rooted in God. So, as you thrive, remember this checkpoint. Come to it often.

Proverbs 3:9 states, "Honour the Lord with thy substance, and with the firstfruits of all thine increase . . ." (KJV). This scripture is often used to explain tithing, but it is much more. God has His will for your life and resources. And just like we have a checkpoint for our heart and mind, this refers to our stuff. Have you asked the Lord what He would like you to do with your possessions and money? Pause for a second. It brings one back to purpose and calling. God has us here for a reason. God's gifts and provision are here for a reason. Thankfully, enjoyment is a result, but this verse talks of bringing the "first fruits of all your increase." In thriving, the leftovers are yours. The first fruits are His. Hallelujah! Remember, your purpose and your calling are in the first fruits. The leading of your family and village are the first fruits. Your home and location are even in the first fruits. Everything that you need is in the first fruits. And then you get to live off the rest. How about that! Do you like those apples?

Proverbs 3:11 states, "My son, despise not the chastening of the Lord; neither be weary of his correction" (KJV). God is faithful to watch over you in the thrive. The scriptures before this one are like checkpoints for your mind, heart, and possessions. This scripture reads more like, "God will be with you watching your moves and caring for you. God will hold you accountable in love and will correct you to help you along the way."

Sometimes God's correction may be hard, but don't look down on it. Pay attention to these moments as gifts. God wants you to enjoy the fullness of His glory, and He will correct you so you can get there. A quick tip that I have learned is that God does not make you do anything. You have a choice in your life; but as you understand God's ways and obey, you find He aids these choices and gives grace when you make mistakes. God sends help through people, thoughts, scripture, examples, ideas, provision, etc. It would not be a good idea to turn up your nose to this; but, in all honesty, everyone has had that moment. The trick is to snap back to reality and realize who God is. In these moments, I think about His creation, wisdom, and power, and I remember how small and unwise I am in comparison. When I think about how much I need this God that created everything, I say, "I'll take the correction."

In the thrive, it is a blessing to find wisdom and get understanding (Proverbs 3:13). Here is the fun part; you—yes, you believer—get to live under the direction of a living God, and you get to learn, live, and experience the goodness of God. You can experience God continually and enjoy this growth by adding wisdom and understanding to your life. Psalm 34:8 talks about tasting and seeing that the Lord is good. Wisdom and understanding are like multiple dishes you get to enjoy. They come in assorted styles, variations, and combinations that you get to try. You get to enjoy the seasonings and preparation of each dish. You can choose from breakfast, lunch, dinner, and even your favorite snack. It can nourish you, or you can even enjoy the decadence of certain wisdom and understanding. By this point, you know the source of all things: God, the one whose Son is Jesus Christ, and all are one with the Holy Spirit. You understand that everything flows from God, the base of all the wisdom and understanding you experience.

As you get wisdom and understanding in the thrive, make sure you do not let them depart from you (Proverbs 3:21). Again, this caution to the believer is another reminder not to be wise in your own experience, intellect, and success. Always bring things back to God and His wisdom. There are so many benefits to keeping sound wisdom and understanding before you. And even more, you have the right wisdom because of the God that you get to know. Cleave to God's wisdom and understanding and never let it go.

Life is going to happen as you are thriving. Situations will come up, governments will have their say in the rules that guide their respective countries, and the world will continue to experience conflict, famine, crisis, and natural disasters. When situations come, your thoughts and response can stay secure in the God you serve. Instead of fear, you can exercise empathy and understanding and pray to God about how He would like to use you in certain situations. You do not have to worry or react in ways that are contrary to what God wants. Your total confidence is in this amazing God who gives peace that passes all of your understanding (Philippians 4:6).

God cares about how you treat others in the thrive. Proverbs 3:27-31 talks about a believer's conduct toward others. It mentions not withholding good when it is due. In these verses, it talks about not devising evil towards others. It also brings out the instruction of not fighting against a person that is not fighting with you. It even speaks of not envying abusive leadership. We cannot forget our responsibility to our neighbors, friends, and family in the thrive. With this being said, in the period of thriving there is a great responsibility to uphold the character and behavior of God. In the thrive it is important to become more reliant on the wisdom and knowledge of God. Remember that in the thrive there is a responsibility for never forgetting what God has done. Also, in the thrive there is a greater responsibility of obedience to God. God wants you to thrive in this life and for eternity with Him.

Through the short story of the widow within seven verses of 2 Kings 4, I hope that each reader has learned the power of seeking and obeying God for every situation. The story does not seem to go beyond this account, but based on the obedience that the widow showed unto God there is no doubt that she did exactly what was instructed and that she and her family thrived. My prayer in you reading this account is that you seek God for your situations and beyond your situation and that you trust him with what is in your hand. I pray that once you make it to the other side of your situation that you glory in God and that you continue to seek a deeper knowledge and relationship with the true and living God.

Take a moment to Reflect

Write your thoughts, questions, or what you have learned in this chapter:

Notes

1. Murphy, Tonja. "My Faith: Lessons from a Widow Woman." Ledger. Mississippi Clarion Ledger, August 26, 2017. https://www.clarionledger.com/story/magnolia/faith/2017/08/26/my-faith-lessons-widow-woman/595808001/. (Accessed: December 14, 2022).

2. *Life Application Study Bible, KJV*. Wheaton, Illinois: Tyndale House Publishers, 1997, 2016, p. 1081 3.3

Acknowledgments

I want to take this moment to thank God for finishing this work. It is the beginning of many. My heart is full as I complete these words and this work.

I also want to thank my family. I thank my wonderful husband, Darnell for allowing me the provision and space to exert God's purpose for my life. I thank my mother, Cheryl Woods for her encouragement throughout the years, for always believing in what God is going to do in my life, and for instructing me in the ways of Christ. Your honest and straightforward profession of faith has eternal repercussions, for which I thank God continually. I thank my dad, Thomas Woods for blessing my life in the way he does and making me take Christ very seriously from an early age. I want to thank my brothers for being protectors and surrogate parents when my parents had to work hard to keep life going. I thank my sister, Keshia, for being wise beyond her years and a constant sounding board for my ideas. I thank God for my niece and nephews, who constantly witness Auntie's quirks and still love me.

There also is a host of friends and family that I cannot thank enough for making this dream happen. I give special thanks to HeartLife Publications (proverbs31cjw@yahoo.com) for being willing to take on my first work and being the best publisher in my eyes. I also want to thank Denise Gates (denisegates@gmail.com) for her editorial expertise.

Finally, I thank you, the reader, for taking the time to purchase my book (the vessel) and read it to its completion (the work), and I pray that God uses it (the oil) to bless your life continually.

About the Author

Ayita Burks is a lover of God and an encourager of every believer. A native of Illinois, Ayita is a graduate of Iowa State University, in Communications, and a longtime servant leader. You can find her cheering believers on daily through digital media, worship, and creative Christian fun. For more information scan here:

MORE BOOKS FROM

Heartlife Publications

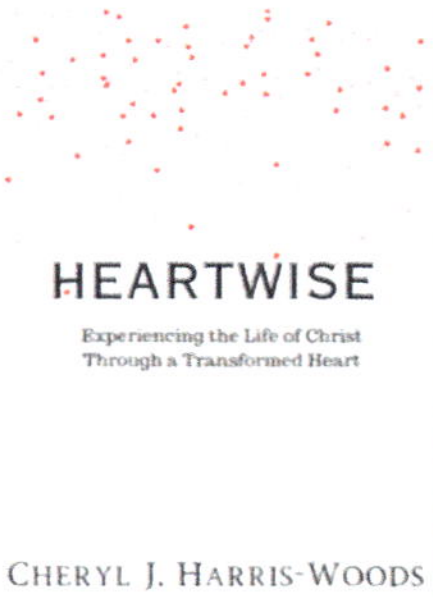

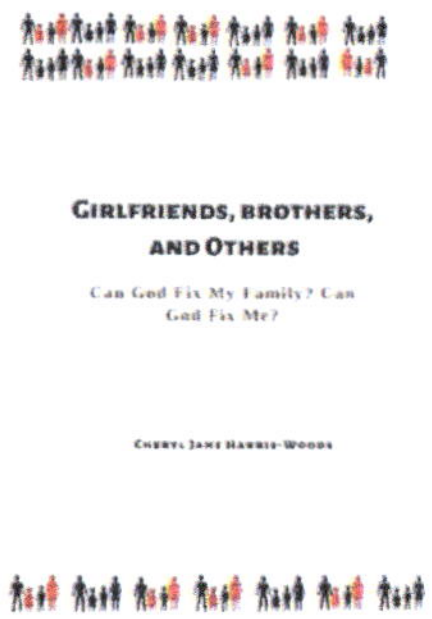

Visit

HEARTLIFEPUBLICATIONS.COM

SCAN ME

Made in the USA
Monee, IL
03 November 2026

67378960R00046